Douglas Garofalo

Joseph Rosa
The Art Institute of Chicago / Yale University Press
A+D SERIES

A+D SERIES

Douglas Garofalo has been published in conjunction with an exhibition of the same title organized by and presented at the Art Institute of Chicago from June 15 to October 8, 2006.

The exhibition is funded by the Fellows of the Department of Architecture and Design with ongoing support from the Architecture and Design Society.

This is a publication of the Ernest R. Graham Study Center for Architectural Drawing at the Art Institute of Chicago.

First edition
Printed in the United States of America

Library of Congress Control Number: 2006926572
ISBN–13 978-0-300-12058-5
ISBN–10 0-300-12058-3

Published by
The Art Institute of Chicago
111 South Michigan Avenue
Chicago, Illinois 60603-6404
www.artic.edu

Distributed by
Yale University Press
302 Temple Street
P.O. Box 209040
New Haven, Connecticut 06520-9040
www.yalebooks.com

Produced by the Publications Department of the Art Institute of Chicago, Susan F. Rossen, Executive Director
Edited by Robert V. Sharp, Director of Publications
Production by Sarah E. Guernsey, Associate Director of Publications
Photography research by Sarah K. Hoadley, Photography Editor
Series design: 2 x 4, New York
Book design by Jeff Wonderland, Associate Director, Department of Graphic Design, Photographic, and Communication Services
Separations by Professional Graphics, Rockford, Illinois
Printing and binding by Lake County Press, Waukegan, Illinois

Photography Credits
Unless otherwise noted, all images are courtesy Garofalo Architects, Inc.
Page 9, photograph ©Roberto Schezen/Esto

Contents

Foreword

It was with great pleasure that we announced just one year ago the appointment of Joseph Rosa as the John H. Bryan Curator of Architecture and Design and charged him with leading an expanded Department of Architecture and Design in ways that would continue the Art Institute's proven commitment to Chicago's remarkable architectural legacy, while also collecting, exhibiting, and publishing broadly on modern and contemporary design practice. I want to acknowledge the work of Joseph Rosa in launching a new series of publications—of which this is the premier installment—and inaugurating his tenure here with this examination of the work of Chicago architect Douglas Garofalo, one of the foremost practitioners of digital design. Joseph Rosa was ably assisted by Carissa Kowalski Dougherty, who also contributed the project descriptions to this catalogue, and other staff in the department including Collection Manager Lori Boyer and volunteers Craig Lee and Harvey Choldin. In addition we wish to express our gratitude to Douglas Garofalo and the other members of Garofalo Architects, including Elaine Fitzgerald, Grant Gibson, Una Moon, Andrew Schachman, Louis Shell, and Chris Wolf, for their cooperation in the realization of this exhibition.

For their work on the exhibition catalogue, I would like to acknowledge members of the Publications Department: Robert V. Sharp, Director, who edited this book; Associate Director Sarah E. Guernsey, who saw to its exacting production standards; and Photography Editor Sarah K. Hoadley, who secured all the images within. The design of the catalogue was conceived by 2 X 4, New York, and was splendidly executed by Jeff Wonderland, Associate Director of Graphic Design, Photographic, and Communication Services. We are grateful to Lyn DelliQuadri, Executive Director of the Graphic Design Department, and the other members of her staff for their work on the installation graphics and materials. As always, the Museum Registration Department under Mary Solt, in particular Darrell Green, Registrar for Loans and Exhibitions, was invaluable in handling the transportation of models and other exhibition items. Various members of the Conservation staff—Barbara Hall, Emily Heye, Barbara Korbel, Harriet Stratis, and Kristi Dahm—gave the exhibition objects their serious attention. We are most thankful to John Molini and Craig Cox and the shipping and installation staff of Museum Registration for their safe treatment and presentation of the works of art, and to Bill Foster and Ray Carlson for their handling of the audio-visual elements in the exhibition. The Kisho Kurokawa Gallery of the Department of Architecture and Design has recently undergone some essential refreshening; we are grateful to William Caddick and Thomas Barnes, the Executive Director and Associate Director, respectively, of the Department of Physical Plant, and their staff for the attention they have given to this space.

Our appreciation also goes to Carrie Heinonen, Vice President for Marketing and Public Affairs, and Erin Hogan, Director of Public Affairs, for their promotion of this exhibition to a growing audience interested in architecture and design. For their diligence in overseeing all our exhibitions, I wish to express our gratitude to Executive Director Ray Van Hook and his staff in the Department of Protection Services. In the critical area of financial support, we are extremely grateful to the Fellows of the Department of Architecture and Design, as well as to the long-standing support of the Architecture and Design Society, Karen Lilly Mozer, President. And for his continuing and generous support of the Department of Architecture and Design, I thank Harold Schiff. Finally, in the Office of the President and Director, I want to thank Dorothy Schroeder, Associate Director for Exhibitions and Museum Administration; Jeanne Ladd, Vice President for Museum Finances; and Dawn Koster, Museum Fiscal Affairs Coordinator. They are vital in making all our plans a reality.

James Cuno
President and Eloise W. Martin Director
The Art Institute of Chicago

5

Spatial Clarities and Formal Complexities: The Architecture of Douglas Garofalo by Joseph Rosa

The proliferation of digital literacy in architectural practice since the early 1990s has made theory instructional, informing new methods of both conceptualization and construction and resulting in new building ideologies.[1] Chicago-based architect Douglas Garofalo is one of the country's leaders in bringing digital pedagogy into the practice of architecture, and he is also one of the most prolific designers in this genre with a broad range of projects and completed works. The work of his studio, Garofalo Architects, illustrates how these new architectural frontiers have widened, fusing with other media to carry forward varying aesthetic explorations and generating new typologies that are changing the way architecture is fabricated, aestheticized, and perceived in the twenty-first century.

Douglas Garofalo was born in upstate New York in 1958. In 1976 he enrolled at the University of Notre Dame—then known for its progressive ideology grounded in modern architecture—and received his bachelor's degree in architecture in 1981. Upon graduating he moved to the Seattle/Vancouver area and worked for William Graham Architects and Planners for two years before relocating to Chicago. In the offices of Kessler, Merci Architects and then Solomon, Cordwell, Buenz Architects, he spent two more years—during which time he received his professional license to practice in the

Fig. 1 Camouflage House study 7

state of Illinois—and in 1985 decided to pursue a graduate degree in architecture at Yale University. One of his reasons for selecting that school's architecture program was its proximity to the university's art school—at the time located in the same building. Garofalo's work reflects his strong interest in artistic practices and methodologies that inform his own architectural production, which has always been very tactile in character. Completing his M.Arch. in 1987, he returned to Chicago to establish his own practice and accepted a teaching appointment at the University of Illinois at Chicago. Today Garofalo is a full professor there. Since 1994 he has taught at Chicago's Archeworks, an alternative design laboratory for students and practitioners with a commitment to social responsibility.

By the early 1990s Garofalo had received a series of commissions for additions to houses, and, of this group, his 1990 Skokie, 1991 Winnetka, and 1993 Highland Park residences—all in Illinois—showcased a bold vocabulary of collaged forms that were aesthetically experimental in character while remaining formal in relation to the existing conditions of each house and its respective site. His unbuilt theoretical 1991 Camouflage House, however, illustrates a strong ideological framework that can be seen in many later projects that have come to fruition (fig. 1). Designed for a housing development on a descending site in Burr Ridge, a western suburb of Chicago, the house is conceptually designed around the driveway, an expression of the central role and controlling character of the automobile in suburban environments. The effort at camouflage—intended to conceal the house in the landscape—is an ironic commentary on the ever-growing proliferation of built structures within the natural landscape. The aesthetic character of the building's exterior would be collaged in a variety of materials from metals and woods to synthetic resins. While intended to conceal itself, the Camouflage House actually pays homage in its treatment of spatial conditions to an architectural icon that is also hidden from view in the hills of Capri, Italy: the 1940 Villa Malaparte (fig. 2).[2] The most visible element of Garofalo's design is the stairlike massing at the approach to the Camouflage House, which is very reminiscent of the stepped ascent to the roof of the villa designed by the Italian Rationalist architect Adalberto Libera (1903–1963) for the writer Curzio Malaparte (1898–1957). Well-known for its siting, which offers breathtaking views—and only accessible by foot—Villa Malaparte is perched on Punta Massullo on the eastern side of the isle of Capri, and it literally becomes an extension of this terraced landscape in the transition from stairs to viewing platform. Access to the house is gained through a discreet entrance located at the side of the property.

Fig. 2 Adalberto Libera, Villa Malaparte, Capri, Italy, 1940

Garofalo's multimedia representation of the Camouflage House also reflects his interest in visual tropes to resituate and rethink architecture. While a simple wooden model was made of the house, another one was produced with the painted characteristics of camouflage. From above the latter of these, the house is indistinguishable from its landscape, though elevational views reveal the form rising up from its two-dimensional camouflage patterning. Garofalo's collage box, which contains a site plan model and drawings, recalls shadow boxes by the artist Joseph Cornell (1903–1973). This project's comprehensive, subversive ideology is completed by the site plan, which traditionally is accompanied by text that spells out the boundaries of the land configuration. Here, however, that text concerns the intention of camouflage deployment and the social histories of humankind. This level of textual poetic play also appears in the legend for the plans of the house, for there Garofalo has labeled rooms as "anonymous," "scenic overlook," and "private." The Camouflage House demonstrates the architect's theoretical approach—devoid of the rhetoric—and it illustrates his ability to create new avant-garde designs with spatial experiences that share affinities and principles with historical examples of twentieth-century modern architecture.

Spatial complexity is central to all of Garofalo's designs that are generated from tactile conditions that evolve into dynamic enclosures. His 1995–98 Markow Residence, for example, marks the arrival of digital production methodologies in his studio, and it is one of the first realized houses that employed this technology (fig. 3). Described by Garofalo as a "transitional project in [his] studio," because it witnessed the shift in his office from tactile formal investigations to a more fluid process of digital modeling vis-à-vis computer software, the house reveals the evidence of this change in its bold massing. While Garofalo's earlier residential work was more collaged in character, the street façade here is quite aggressive: a hovering, curved surface that visually inserts the house into its homogeneous suburban fabric while announcing its difference. Although the project is an addition to an existing, split-level ranch house, Garofalo's modifications and additions are most evident at the front of the dwelling where curved and canted forms contrast with the only true vertical surfaces, namely, the garage and front door. The modulated, compound, bulbous curved forms that compose this street façade at first appear to arise from an animation. These forms illustrate a change in Garofalo's architectural vocabulary as it becomes more fluid while still retaining his interest in saturated bold colors to articulate such shapes.

While the Markow House can be considered one of the first digitally informed residential projects in architecture to be realized, it is Garofalo's collaboration with Greg Lynn and Michael McInturf that truly changed the course of digital ideology in the built world. The 1996–99 Korean Presbyterian Church of New York located in Sunnyside, Queens, the result of this joint venture, set a new precedent for what digitally literate studios could achieve with Garofalo in Chicago, McInturf in Cincinnati, and Lynn in New Jersey and, later, California. Through a proliferation of e-mails and data sent back and forth electronically, this collaborative team pooled their resources to conceive, fabricate, and build a church that comprises a surprisingly large program: a main sanctuary accommodating 2,500 people for services, a 600-seat wedding chapel, a 1,000-seat cafeteria, 80 classrooms, and a daycare center. Aesthetically, the Korean Presbyterian Church is a vast series of parasitical forms that together almost encase a defunct 1932 Art Deco building that formerly housed

Fig. 3 Markow Residence

the Knickerbocker Laundry Factory. The character of this existing structure is revealed in portions of the façade and in the interior clear spans of the sanctuary.

The church is one of the earliest and largest examples of digital ideology taking place in architecture. While some of the early digital modeling images of the project might, in retrospect, appear primitive in comparison to today's highly developed digital techniques, when this building was designed and built it was the most avant-garde example of digital literacy transitioning from its pedagogical roots into the realm of critical practice. At the time, however, the simple act of using digitally informed machinery to crimp the edge of a building material was not hugely feasible. Hence its bulbous, angular massing. While it was hailed as the "first blob," the formal characteristics of this church were in fact much more a composition of folds and bends deployed over and around the simple rectilinear massing of the original factory structure.[3]

One of the best examples of Garofalo's penchant for spatial conditions that generate complex formal conditions —filtered through a more developed digital literacy—can be seen in the firm's 1999 LOESS System Transitional Housing project (fig 4). Designed in collaboration with Randall Kober, this conceptual project was intended to fill the need to provide housing for homeless individuals who are

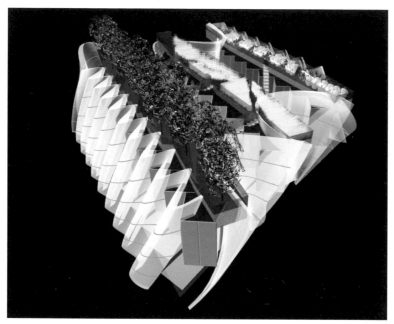

Fig. 4 LOESS System Transitional Housing

transitioning to more secure living conditions. The LOESS housing is essentially a shelter, reminiscent of a small, walled-in city, with spaces for living, working, and relaxing. A transparent, sinuously folded surface wraps around the site's perimeter to screen various programmatic functions, whether this means public space at the ground level, single-occupancy housing units at the second level, or a terraced landscape at the third. Conceptually, the project is designed to act as a ready-made that can be deployed in a vacant lot of virtually any shape. The overall matrix for this three-story complex is generated through digital modeling from a single module that is rotated up from the first floor (reserved for retail at the perimeter) to the second floor (where it becomes the single-room-occupancy units) and then up to the third (where these modules become three long, linear surfaces that house gardens for the occupants). The trace of this rotating form can be seen in the surface of the folded perimeter wall.

As with the LOESS housing, which employed sensuously curved surfaces to enclose this multifunctional transitional housing, a similar methodology in the deployment of irregular planes can be seen in two projects that Garofalo Architects undertook in Wisconsin: the 2000–03 Manilow Residence in Spring Prairie and the 2002–04 Nothstine Residence in Green Bay. Located on a 75-acre site, the Manilow property offered a vast rambling former farmhouse. Garofalo added to the juxtaposition of existing roof profiles—which from a distance visually reads as an assembly of freestanding red and orange structures—a large, two-story addition that is his first non-Cartesian building form. Though his creation is essentially a blob, the interior of this form is beautifully articulated with a second-floor bedroom that looks out onto the landscape. To produce this complex structure, plywood ribs were laser-cut and assembled to create the sculptural massing. The architects then clad this compound curved roof structure—which cascades down from the roof eaves to the deck on the ground floor—with diamond-shaped shingles made of titanium to give the overall contiguous surface a scalelike appearance.

The sinuous roof plane of the Manilow Residence appears to have nestled down upon the vast assembly of barnlike forms, while the Nothstine Residence—designed around the same time—incorporates a yellow, ribbonlike fiberglass form that visually wraps the building. This ribbon-wrapped enclosure cantilevers out from the house, just as it protrudes into the existing rectilinear massing of the house, which is situated on a steep, sloping site. This folded form also demarcates the vast areas of transparency throughout the house. While not always directly visible, this dynamic fold bends through the house from its lowest level to its roof. The spatial implications from this folded fiberglass form are breathtaking.

In most of Garofalo's projects the addition to or augmentation of existing structures is celebrated through the simple act of spatial interventions that are visually identifiable. This ideology is very much part of the post-1968 architectural rhetoric—which was, in varying ways, informed by semiotics, linguistics, conceptual art, and film theory.[4] Around this period in the United States, radical avant-garde additions became celebrated appendages to traditionally styled homes in the suburbs. Examples as different as Michael Graves's 1969 Benacerraf House and Peter Eisenman's 1967 House I, both additions to homes in Princeton, New Jersey, might be named, as well as Stanley Tigerman's 1978 addition of a kitchen to a home in the Chicago suburbs—which he dubbed "Kosher Kitchen for a Jewish Princess" and to which he imparted a plan that was round like a bagel—and Frank O. Gehry's 1978–79 addition to his own home in Santa Monica, California.[5] As with Graves, Eisenman, Tigerman, and Gehry—each of whom further developed his own self-referential architectural idiom in later commissions for completely new homes—so too with Douglas Garofalo. His more recent Griffith and Gary houses—both of which are currently under construction—showcase an ideology that generates designs that are meta-narratives of his clients' needs and the sites they present him, but that also results in a contemporary architecture that is distinctive and completely referential.

Situated on a rolling rural site in Decatur, Illinois, the Griffith House, designed for a couple with two sets of twins—one identical, the other fraternal—architecturally manifests a narrative of pairing forms. These two "fraternal" forms, one clad mostly in wood and the other enclosed in glass, are sheltered by a larger rectangular roof plane that visually brings these two geometries together. To differentiate the formal characteristics of these structures further, the wood-clad, undulating, snakelike form is wood framed, while the simpler, rectangular, glass-enclosed form is steel framed. Programmatically, the glass-enclosed pavilion houses the public spaces such as the living room and dining room. While the wood-clad form contains bedrooms, a centrally located kitchen that abuts the "public spaces" of the rectangular pavilion conceptually acts as the hinge between these two different forms.

While the Griffith House becomes a formal architectural manifestation of the client's genealogical condition, Garofalo's conception for the Gary House also addresses notions of duality and the typological character of the site. Taking advantage of a sloping site north of Grand Rapids, Michigan, the Gary House comprises two major forms, one of which is burrowed into the site and holds bedrooms and the garage. The roof of this semirecessed form is a manicured lawn and the only formal landscape intervention at this forested site. The concept of the roof plane as a landscape that conceals its function can be seen in Garofalo's 1991 Camouflage House, which featured a stepped roof plane. The other major form—sited adjacent to the burrowed form—is clad in copper and contains the

Fig.5 Hyde Park Art Center

public spaces: kitchen and living and dining rooms. Although both forms are situated at the same elevation, the copper-clad massing, which cantilevers out, is more sculptural in its plan and sectional characteristics and is separated from the rectangular, burrowed form by a simple, intermediate glass enclosure that acts as the point of entry into the house.

While both the Griffith and Gary residences encompass forms that operate in opposition to each other, they generate a dialogue between these two conditions that result in a larger spatial framework that becomes the dwelling itself. Garofalo employs a similar methodology with his Hyde Park Art Center (2002–06), newly completed on the South Side of Chicago (fig. 5). Established in 1939, the Hyde Park Art Center has provided art exhibitions and programs for the metropolitan Chicago area for decades. The new Art Center is located in a building formerly occupied by the University of Chicago Press. This rather normative, nondescript brick building, however, is being transformed by Garofalo Architects with a simple formal intervention of steel and glass at the entrance that distinguishes the Art Center's new home. This elevated form—which provides a strong identity to the community—is an experimental electronic exhibition space that hovers above the entrance and projects above the roofline of the building. Interior scrims and shades allow this transparent glass façade to become a digital projection screen. Beyond this formal intervention is a vast interior of 38,000 square feet that should provide the Art Center with the amenities it needs to grow into the future.

One of Garofalo's largest spatial interventions is the conceptual Loop Ecologies project (2004–05). For Garofalo, "The elevated Loop train system is one of the most defining moments in downtown Chicago." To celebrate this spatial condition, he proposed constructing a secondary horizontal structure above the tracks that would be demarcated vertically by new stations with public amenities—supple appendages that wrap over, around, and under the existing elevated tracks. On top of this new contiguous rooftop would be a vast, self-sufficient ecological field supporting various crops and such animals as goats and sheep that produce cheese, milk, and wool. New programmable structures would also be parasitical to the Loop's immense transit armature and act as a sound-insulating barrier between the streets and the El. These voids could then be dedicated to a variety of activities that lend themselves to linear programmed spaces for such activities as swimming, bocce ball, and skating, and express bicycle lanes.

The folding together of programs that share spatial characteristics into new relationships is precisely what makes Garofalo's work so progressive in conception and refreshing in its execution. In addition, the juxtaposition between the existing—the elevated loop—and the new—programmed events—that engulfs this simple system of circulation results in an experimental conceptual model that shows Garofalo's continued interest in rethinking the normative conditions and relationships found in architecture.

The pedagogy and practice of architecture has shifted in character over the last decade from tactile methodologies of thinking about buildings to the proliferation of digital literacy in the conception and fabrication of innovative forms. This is changing the course of the discipline for the twenty-first century. To operate in this new frontier it is essential that avant-garde architecture be ideologically grounded in its conception, allowing the subjective character of the architect's intent to operate aesthetically and formally. Douglas Garofalo's career reflects this ideological evolution. While his early residential works showcased a bold architectural vocabulary—that was collaged and additive in character—his more recent, digitally informed projects are more fluid in form, character, and programming. One constant throughout Garofalo's work is his ideology, which is grounded in rethinking the spatial connotations of architecture and its resulting formal characteristics—hence becoming a model for what radical avant-garde thinking in architecture can be in a digitally informed practice.

Notes
This essay is based on interviews and conversations with Douglas Garofalo between fall 2005 and winter 2006.
1. For more on digital architecture and its origins, see Joseph Rosa, **Next Generation Architecture: Folds, Blobs, and Boxes** (Rizzoli International, 2003), the revised version of a text that originally appeared in Joseph Rosa, **Folds, Blobs, and Boxes: Architecture in the Digital Era** (Heinz Architectural Center, Carnegie Museum of Art, Pittsburgh, 2001). See also Frédéric Migayrou, **Non-Standard Architecture** (Centre Pompidou, Paris, 2004) and Branko Kolarevic, ed., **Architecture in the Digital Age: Design and Manufacturing** (Spon Press, 2003).
2. The house was used in Jean-Luc Godard's 1963 film **Contempt** with Bridget Bardot, Jack Palance, Fritz Lang, and Michel Piccoli. For more on Villa Malaparte, see Marida Talamona, **Casa Malaparte** (Princeton Architectural Press, 1992) and Gabriella Belli and Vittorio Gregotti, et al., **Adalberto Libera: Opera Completa** (Edizioni Electa, 1989).
3. Joseph Giovannini, "Computer Worship," **Architecture** (October 1999), pp. 88-99.
4. For more on post-1968 avant-garde ideology, see K. Michael Hays, ed., **Architecture Theory since 1968** (MIT Press, 1998); Peter Eisenman, "Notes on Conceptual Architecture: Towards a Definition," **Casabella** (December 1971), p. 41.
5. For more on these important residential additions, see Mario Gandelsonas, "On Reading Architecture," **Progressive Architecture** (March 1972), pp. 69–74; **Five Architects: Eisenman, Graves, Gwathmey, Hejduk, Meier** (Wittenborn & Company, 1972); Peter Eisenman, Rosalind Krauss, and Manfredo Tafuri, **House of Cards** (Oxford University Press, 1987); Karen Vogel Wheeler, Peter Arnell, and Ted Bickford, ed., **Michael Graves: Buildings and Projects, 1966–1981** (Rizzoli International, 1982); Sarah Mollman, ed., **Stanley Tigerman: Buildings and Projects, 1966–1989** (Rizzoli International, 1989); Francesco Dal Co and Kurt W. Forster, **Frank O. Gehry: The Complete Works** (Phaidon Press, 2003).

Projects

Camouflage House

Burr Ridge, Illinois, 1991

The Camouflage House is a conceptual project for an imagined planned community called Falling Water in Burr Ridge, a western suburb of Chicago. Garofalo's design takes the architectural and aesthetic conventions for such corporate-controlled developments and turns them on their head to emphasize the absurdity of prevailing, idealized notions of landscape and domesticity.

The plan for the Camouflage House exaggerates the idea that the automobile is an integral part of suburban living. Cars are treated like extra family members; the garage is integrated into the room layout as a pivotal programmatic element and the entire house is oriented toward the bifurcated driveway. The seemingly random pattern of colors and materials that cover the house and extend into the landscape emphasize the absurd conceit that a million-dollar house could fit in with its natural surroundings. Here the relationship between the term "natural" and the highly choreographed landscape of suburban America is called into question with a fragmented, "camouflaged" structure that fails to obey the rules of suburban taste.

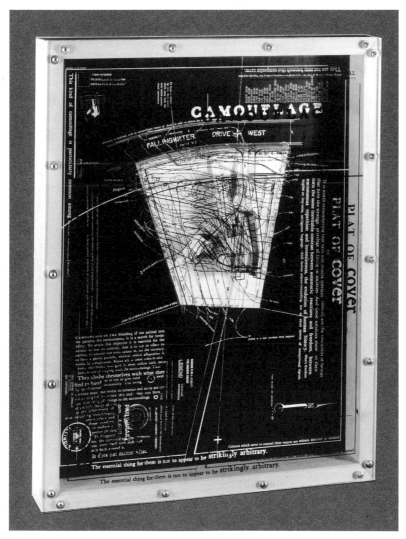

Shadow box presentation of design concept

Following pages:
Above left, view of model
Below left, first-floor plan
Above right, west elevation of model
Below right, south elevation of model

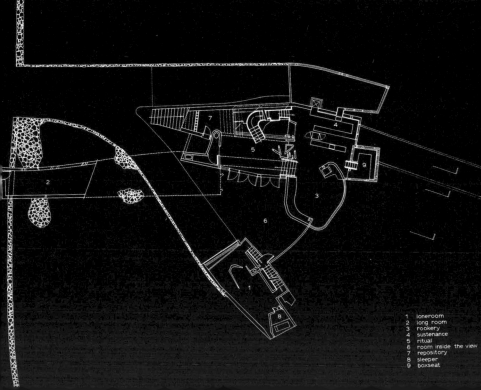

1 loneroom
2 long room
3 rookery
4 sustenance
5 ritual
6 room inside the view
7 repository
8 sleeper
9 boxseat

Markow Residence

Prospect Heights, Illinois, 1995–98

With the Markow Residence, Garofalo again demonstrates his ability to take a suburban housing typology and reinvest it with contextual meaning through new formal strategies. The original split-level house is typical of those found throughout postwar suburban Chicago. But rather than conceal the existing structure, Garofalo chose to maintain the twin-gabled rear and create a dramatically different front façade that emphasizes the home's hybrid nature. The angular, folding roof planes are visible from all sides; metal panels tie the old and new structures together and create a landscape of "vernacular mutation." Boldly colored exterior walls stand out among the more muted hues of other homes in the neighborhood.

Garofalo's addition greatly increases the house's level of complexity in both plan and section. The new volume departs from the orthogonal orientation of the existing spaces, creating an irregular form that rises above the ground level. In the interior, a network of glass walkways and ramps weaves in and out of the structure. Between this circulation space and the two bedrooms that cantilever off the rear of the house, an amorphic, curvilinear bathroom/utility core provides a sculptural center than penetrates down to the first floor.

Interior view showing glass walkway

Exterior view of main entrance

Exterior view

Korean Presbyterian Church of New York

With Greg Lynn FORM and Michael McInturf Architects
Queens, New York, 1996–99

The Korean Presbyterian Church of New York (KPCNY) was a collaboration with architectural colleagues Greg Lynn FORM of New Jersey
(now of Venice, California) and Michael McInturf Architects of Cincinnati. In what was a proto-digital project, the architects used tech-
nologies that allowed for both design innovation and breakthrough
communication strategies. The final form is an analog approximation
of "blob" digital-modeling techniques that transformed a regular,
orthogonal box into an irregular, asymmetrical building. The design
process itself was enabled by e-mail, which enhanced the ability to
send design drawings electronically for review by team members in
different parts of the country.

The KPCNY is an adaptive reuse project that took the abandoned
Knickerbocker Laundry Factory in Queens and transformed it into
a religious, educational, and community center for a growing con-
gregation. The team's design is a hybrid, parasitical steel structure
that draws on the rhythms and materials of the old industrial building
and creates a series of telescoping fins along one side, expanding the
sanctuary space and directing the visitor's eyes toward the front of the
church. The existing structure was further modified by the addition of
curving circulation spaces and a steel "shed" enclosure that dramatically altered the roof profile.

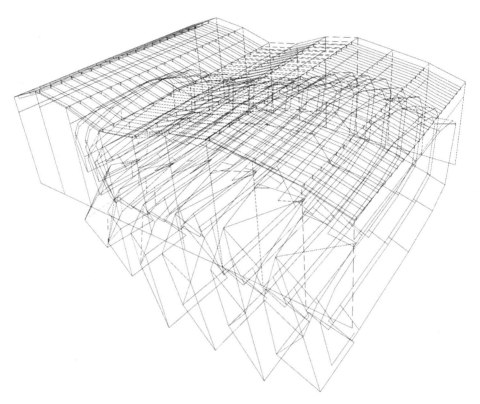

Wireframe schematic diagram of building volume

Top: Exterior view of main entrance
Above: Exterior view of sanctuary

Interior view of sanctuary

Chicago Public School

Chicago, Illinois, 2000–01

Garofalo's entry for the Chicago Public Schools Design Competition demonstrates a topographical approach to architecture, using elements that one might find in a natural landscape to create an accessible system of wayfinding. The 2000–01 "Big Shoulders, Small Schools" competition called for designs on either of two actual sites in the city—one South Side, one North Side—with specific requirements addressing universal design. In Garofalo's proposal, ramps are not concessions made grudgingly to satisfy accessibility requirements, but essential aspects of the building's organization and structure.

All of the programmatic elements are symbolically housed under one undulating, folding roof plane. The design accommodates three small schools-within-a-school, each with its own architectural identity, a structural "tube" distinguished by color and ramp characteristics. The rhythm of these classroom tubes reflects the pattern of the residences across the street, while the circulation and administrative spaces run north–south, parallel to the street. The communal spaces—including a library, computer lab, restrooms, lunchroom, and offices—are envisioned as forms in a landscape, discrete "pods" in the larger framework of the school. This layout allows for the efficient movement of students, who are able to enter their own classroom tube without having to pass through other areas of the school.

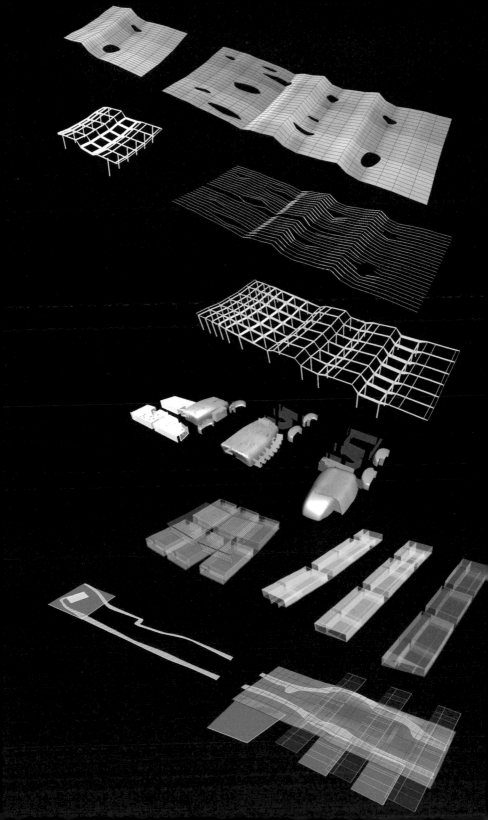

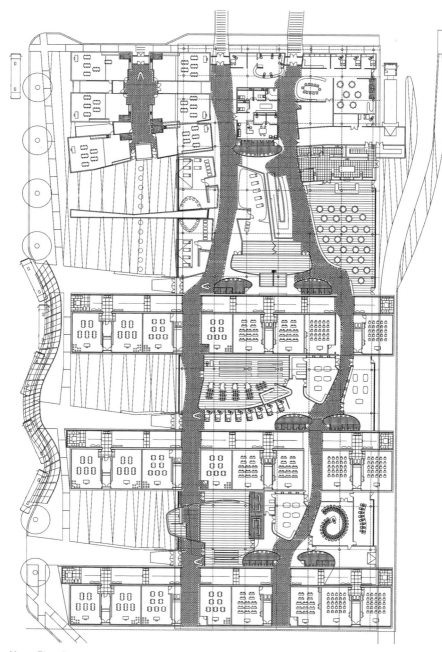

Above: First-floor plan of main building

Preceding page: Exploded axonometric diagram of structure
Opposite page: Site plan showing entire school

Manilow Residence

Spring Prairie, Wisconsin, 2000–03

The additions to the Manilow Residence were designed as a small village for the members of an extended family who use the property in Spring Prairie, Wisconsin, as a rural retreat. Each built element has its own individual identity while still participating in a larger set of relationships that are tied together by the use of color and material. At one end of the large, rambling house, Garofalo added several rooms, including a kitchen, dining room, master bedroom, and two children's bedrooms. He also constructed, on other parts of the property, a small llama barn and a tool shed with a screened porch looking out over the garden.

    The most radical of the alterations was the introduction of a sinuous, titanium-clad roof structure that encloses the new wing and begins to wrap around the original building. While Garofalo maintained the vertical wooden siding so familiar from numerous barns dotting the Wisconsin landscape, the titanium shell departs from the vernacular, interrupting the gable pattern and transforming one end of the house into a distinct "other." The plywood ribs that compose the structural members were produced entirely by computer-numerically-controlled (CNC) milling. Each undulating curve has a unique shape that is determined in the digital design process. The interior is just as meticulously detailed; the wooden structure is revealed and offset by smooth swaths of burnished plaster.

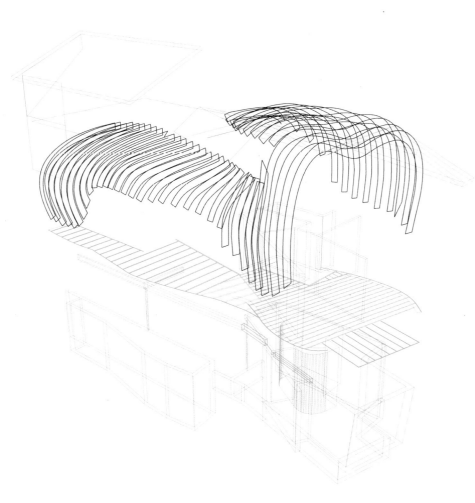

Exploded axonometric diagram of structure

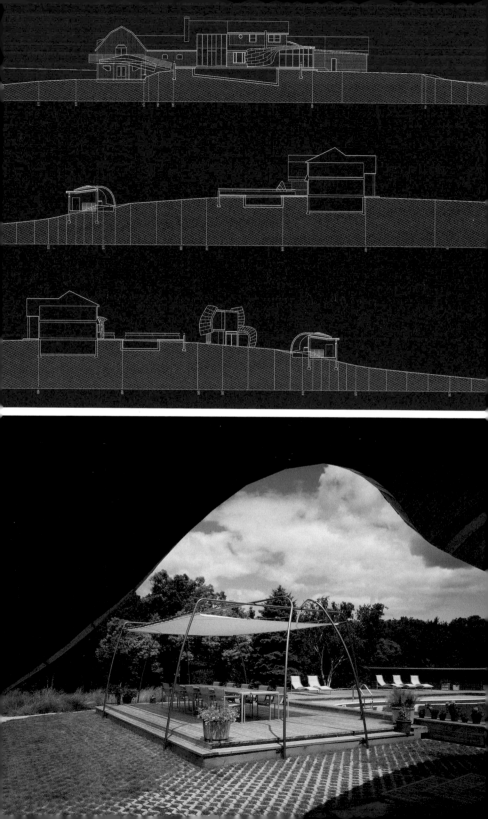

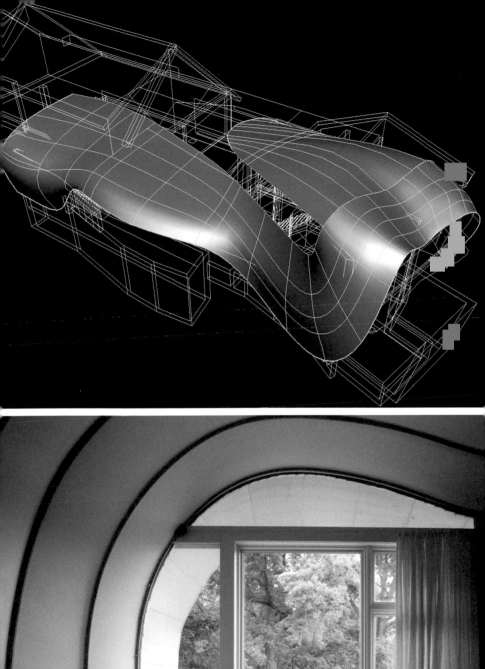

Exterior view

Preceding pages:
Above left: Site sections
Below left: View from living room
out to terrace and pool
Above right: Wireframe schematic
diagram of building volume
Below right: Interior view of bedroom

ABLA Homes

Chicago, Illinois, 2001

Garofalo's entry for the 2001 competition sponsored by the National Endowment for the Arts for the redevelopment of the Chicago Housing Authority's ABLA Homes created an innovative housing solution without resorting to either sterile, modernist apartment complexes or New Urbanist pastiches of a traditional streetscape. Instead of attempting to fashion an artificial sense of "community" via aesthetics or forced behavioral patterns, Garofalo treats the block as an ecosystem in which community develops through variation and coexistence. This urban ecology is accomplished by diversifying the layout of individual units, making their appearance consistent, and emphasizing the physical and conceptual relationships between them.

The ABLA project demonstrates how a mixed-income housing development composed of standardized elements can be designed to appear nonrepetitive and unique. While the design utilizes modular and premanufactured elements to reduce cost and construction time, the overall effect is one of material and formal complexity. The façade of the mixed-income development is divided into three distinct material zones: a lower stratum of concrete and a continuous midsection band of brick, topped by more open, glazed, third-story towers. Connections are made horizontally through ground-level circulation and a second-floor communal green space that spans the alley and creates an elevated central plaza.

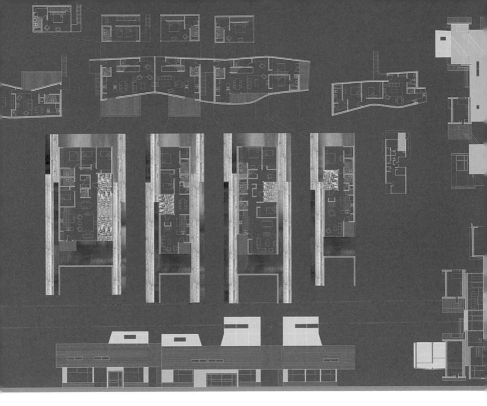

Plans and elevations

precast concrete panels

prefabricated steel components

engineered lumber

Top: Roosevelt Road elevation
Above: Construction sequencing diagrams

brick ribbons

window and wall panels

MCA: Between the Museum and the City

Chicago, Illinois, 2001–02

Garofalo's temporary installation in the plaza fronting the main entrance to the Museum of Contemporary Art established a critical connection between the rigid, orthogonal museum structure and the city's public space. Working with students from a class at the University of Illinois at Chicago, Garofalo designed the installation to activate the cold, sterile plaza and create a complex backdrop for urban activities. A series of pavilions, assembled from disparate materials, provided a gathering place for passersby and museum-goers while simultaneously functioning as a piece of art in the spirit of the Young Architects Program jointly sponsored by the Museum of Modern Art and the P.S. 1 Contemporary Art Center of New York.

A dynamic, spiderlike system of steel armatures extended down the stairs of the museum, defining the outdoor space and providing a scaffold for other elements of the structure. Garofalo's concept of weaving together the urban fabric is manifested in this project's complex, interlacing forms and in the "soft islands" that were woven together with yellow polyethylene gas pipe, cables, cellular foam, and bungee cords. Because the installation could not be permanently affixed to the plaza, Garofalo and his team designed concrete anchors and specialized hardware to withstand the heavy wind loads on the site without giving the overall structure an overbearing feeling of heaviness. Other materials, including yellow fabric and dimensional lumber, provided tactile and textural contrasts to the more industrial materials.

View of installation, looking east
toward the museum

Following pages:
Above: Truss/canopy diagrams
Below: Aerial view of installation

Nothstine Residence

Green Bay, Wisconsin, 2002–04

The forms for the additions to the Nothstine Residence in Green Bay, Wisconsin, were derived from the owners' interests in bird watching, horticulture, and slot car racing. Garofalo, for example, designed a long, narrow walkway leading out from the house and passing through midair to provide an ideal vantage point for bird watching. The residents may also choose to be a little bit closer to nature by walking on a landscaped path that follows a stream as it wends its way down the side of the steeply sloping site. The continuous yellow band that weaves in and out of the house is reminiscent of the twisting, circuitous course of a slot car track. Its bright, smooth, fiberglass surface contrasts with the corrugated metal cladding and envelops the new volumes, at one point jutting out above the ground plane and providing spectacular views toward Lake Michigan. The bent structures were constructed using a combination of traditional hand carpentry and computer-numerically-controlled (CNC) milling techniques. Curved steel trusses, generated directly from the design software, were spaced with wood spanning members, after which the entire assembly was sheathed in plywood to give it rigidity and stability.

Interior view of living room with "orb" fireplace

Top: Exterior view at night
Above: Wireframe schematic diagrams
of building volume

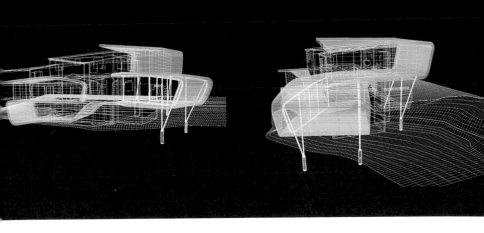

Interior view of living room

Hyde Park Art Center

Chicago, Illinois, 2002–06

Garofalo's largest built work to date is the expansion and rehabilita-
tion of an old University of Chicago Press building for the new home
of the Hyde Park Art Center. The 35,000-square-foot adaptive reuse
project houses visual art galleries, studios, and educational space on
a site adjacent to the Metra commuter rail tracks in Chicago's Hyde
Park neighborhood. The overall design enhances the mission of the
nonprofit arts organization by creating a strong visual identity and
enabling the building to interact with visitors and passersby.

The industrial building was given several new faces with which to
address the neighboring streets. Public entrances are marked with
glass-and-steel panels that extend above the two-story structure
and create a landmark for those passing by on the street or on the
train. One of these façade additions becomes an active exhibition
space, cantilevering out from the old brick structure. Through integrated digital projection screens, the surface itself can be used
for viewing experimental and electronic art, while the silhouettes
of visitors inside the gallery add a dynamic element for pedestrians
outside. On the ground level, Garofalo opens the building to its large,
original bays, bringing natural light into the gallery and initiating
connections to the community. The building's "fifth façade"—its roof
plane, visible from nearby residential towers—will be transformed
with the introduction of a prairie landscape.

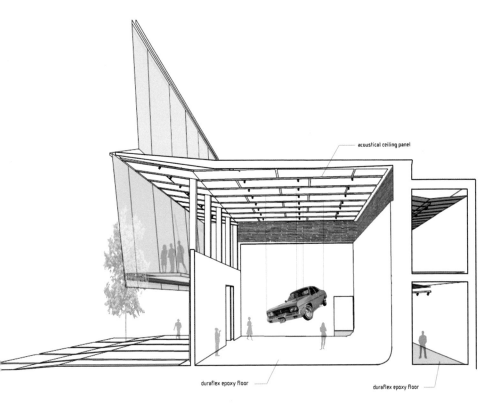

acoustical ceiling panel

duraflex epoxy floor

duraflex epoxy floor

Cross section through gallery

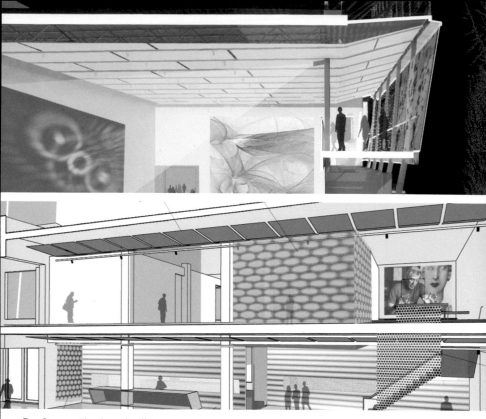

Top: Cross section through gallery
Above: Cutaway perspective view of interior

Exterior perspective rendering of façade at night

Pedestrian Bridge

Chicago, Illinois, 2003

The Pedestrian Bridge Competition entry was a response to a brief from the City of Chicago's Department of Transportation calling for new bridges where North Avenue, 35th Street, and 41st and 43rd streets meet Lake Shore Drive at the city's lakefront. The bridges were to be not only elevated pathways for pedestrians and bicyclists but also structures that provide strong visual cues for through traffic on Lake Shore Drive. Garofalo's scheme emphasizes the connections that a bridge makes with the ground; his structure extends into the landscape and responds to the different conditions on either side of the busy thoroughfare. The approaches are gently sloping mounds that incorporate elements of dune landscapes, prairie grasses, trees, and lighting that then "grow" into the spanning structure of the bridge.

As a living link between the city and the lakefront, the bridge's design recognizes the possibilities for a changing urban landscape. The bridge concept is not only able to change with varying flows of people and potentially shifting uses, but also adapt to different site conditions. A flexible cladding system allows the structure to remain open to the elements or to accommodate any level of enclosure, including a scheme that employs photovoltaic panels to provide power to light the walkway.

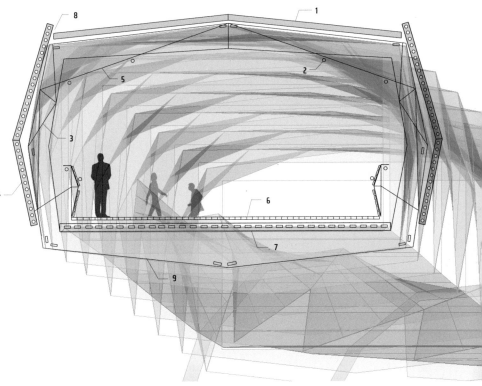

Cross section showing construction elements:
1) translucent panels; 2) LED lights; 3) secondary
support for cladding; 4) perforated metal cladding; 5)
steel diagonal spanning elements; 6) wood deck with
integrated LED lighting; 7) waterproof deck; 8) drain-
age; 9) steel structural section

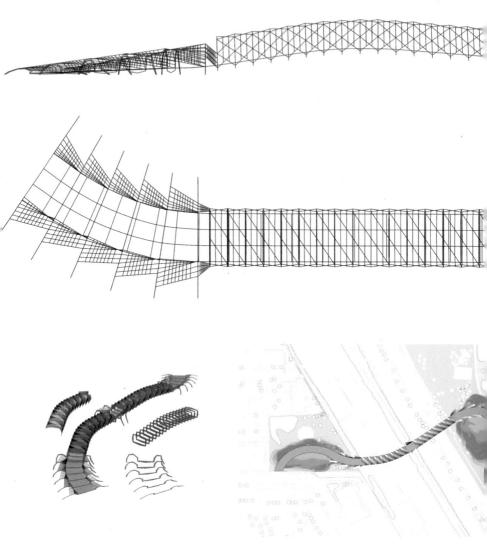

Top: Elevation
Middle: Plan
Bottom: Exploded axonometric
diagram of structure, and site plan

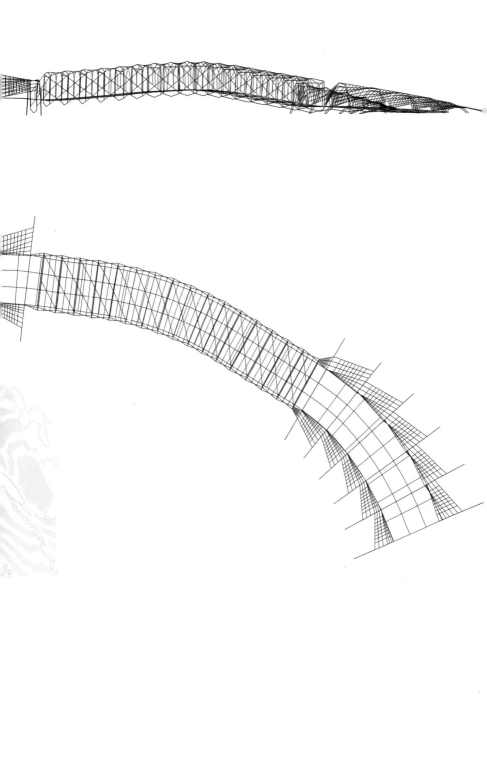

Ford Calumet Environmental Center

with Xavier Vendrell Studio
Chicago, Illinois, 2003–04

The Ford Calumet Environmental Center is a competition entry for a proposed educational facility on an old manufacturing site in Chicago's far southeast side Hegewisch neighborhood. The landscape has been largely reclaimed by native and nonnative vegetation—but contains significant remnants of its industrial past. Garofalo's competition entry, a collaboration with Xavier Vendrell Studio of Chicago, uses the idea of filtering as a conceptual basis for the design. The building mediates between visitor and landscape, interior and exterior conditions, while attempting to preserve the site's delicate web of natural and constructed environments.

The proposed environmental center holds the southeast corner of the site with a gently angled shape that provides a long public façade to the access roads. Visitors are filtered in through the main volume and then dispersed out over the landscape in slender peninsulas of cantilevered gallery space. Natural light is brought into the galleries through large, glazed openings screened with irregularly perforated metal. The resulting patterns of light and shadow are intended to resemble something found in nature—a sun-dappled forest floor or the bottom of a creek bed. The permeability of the structure is further emphasized by light wells that punctuate the space and create a visual dialogue between interior and exterior.

Aerial perspective rendering of
main entrance

Richmond Center for Visual Arts

Kalamazoo, Michigan, 2003–04

The Richmond Center for Visual Arts is a new building for the College of Fine Arts at Western Michigan University that includes gallery space, an auditorium, classrooms, and common areas. The overall project also encompasses the renovation of an adjacent building—which formerly served as engineering laboratories and classrooms—into studio and office facilities. Garofalo's work, which was taken through design development, uses varying materials and opacities to distinguish among the programmatic functions of the space.

The façade of the addition extends into the heart of the WMU campus, completing the College of Fine Arts quadrangle and establishing the sculptural form of the Richmond Center as a new focal point. The rectilinear, glass-clad lobby is contrasted with the curving, opaque surface of the metal-clad auditorium, which in turn offsets the heavy, brick structure of the former engineering hall. The glazed spaces extend their formal vocabulary to the old building as they begin to wrap around the brick-and-concrete mass. Another connection between the two volumes is established with a horizontal band of clerestory windows on the second level—a circulation and lighting solution that enabled the university to maintain an existing access road and allows the galleries to take advantage of the natural light.

Exterior perspective rendering
showing main entrance

Top and above: Aerial perspective
renderings

Exterior perspective rendering showing
outer wall of auditorium

Gary Residence

Ada, Michigan, 2004–06

This house, set in a rural area of western Michigan, is one of Garofalo's first ground-up projects. One of the requirements for the Gary Residence was to minimize the building's apparent impact on the heavily wooded, secluded site. The house is broken into two distinct volumes: one buried in the sloping ground, the other hovering at the level of the forest canopy. In the former, the house becomes literally embedded in the site, distinguished from the surrounding woodland groundcover with a patch of manicured lawn covering the roof. The more private and utilitarian aspects of the home—such as the bedrooms, storage, and laundry—are located in this volume. The semipublic spaces of the kitchen, dining room, and living room are housed in the sculptural, copper-clad volume that projects out into the trees.

Other features also enhance the inhabitants' connection with their natural surroundings. Large, glazed areas, for example, provide the west-facing rooms with views out over the site. A walkway projects from the facade, jutting out even further into the landscape; this long, narrow outlook recalls a similar feature from Garofalo's treatment of the Nothstine Residence. An underground tunnel leads from the depths of the house's interior to a small deck further down the hillside.

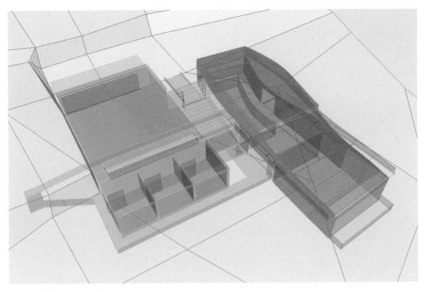

Axonometric schematic drawing

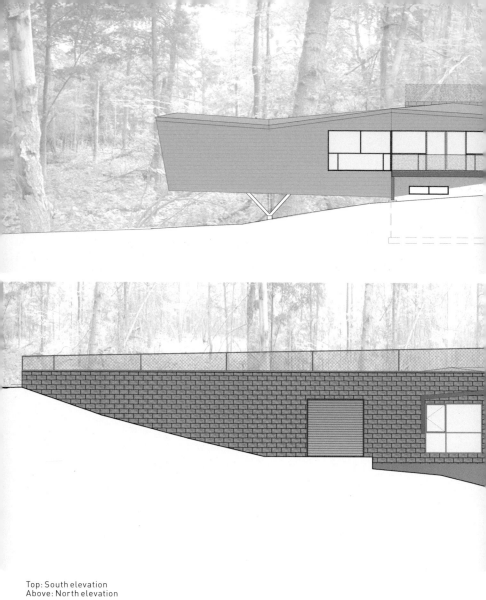

Top: South elevation
Above: North elevation

Griffith Residence

Decatur, Illinois, 2004–06

The design for the Griffith Residence embodies the notion of "doubling"—an appropriate theme for the home of a family with two sets of twins. Here, as in the development of fraternal twins, aspects of form are repeated but clearly differentiated, creating relationships of opposition as well as likeness. Two main volumes make up Garofalo's design, with the kitchen serving as the pivotal point for the house's program. But while the semipublic spaces are enclosed in a strict, rectilinear box, the private spaces and bedrooms reside in a bent, irregular form that is oriented toward views of the surrounding farmland. The former is largely transparent, surrounded by glass; the latter is more opaque, covered in wood. The entire single-story structure is tied together with a folding, undulating metal roof that complements the rolling, rural landscape of the southern Illinois site.

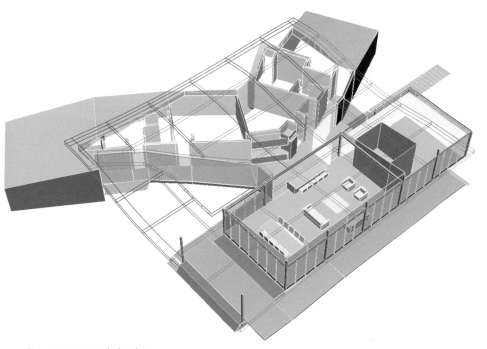

Cutaway axonometric drawing

Exterior view of house under construction

New Loop Ecologies

Chicago, Illinois, 2004–05

New Loop Ecologies is a speculative, urban-scale design project that celebrates the well-known "Loop" in downtown Chicago created by its intersecting elevated train lines with a series of integrated, innovative, and sustainable public sites. The existing tracks are treated as a host structure from which new programs arise and upon which new landscapes are planted; the old industrial city is merged with—but not supplanted by—a greener sensibility. The centrifugal infrastructure that shuttles travelers off to Chicago's far-flung neighborhoods is thus transformed into a centripetal hub that creates nodes of new public space and concentrates a variety of activities downtown.

Garofalo's design can be viewed as a complex biosystem whose members depend on one another to support diverse, complementary functions. On the street level, a linear arcade separates automobiles and pedestrian traffic from the tracks overhead. This zone may accommodate a number of public amenities, including lap swimming lanes, bocce ball courts, bicycle lanes, and exhibition spaces. Above the tracks a band of agricultural landscape provides a continuous link between elements. This green space is a pragmatic and aesthetic addition: the landscape supports consumer and feed crops as well as grazing sheep and goats that would provide milk, cheese, and wool. Periodic programmatic interventions, including small business incubator sites, restaurants, nightclubs, and tourist information centers, protrude up through the top layer, signaling the activities below and creating new densities in the central cityscape.

Exterior perspective rendering of CTA station

Following pages:
Above left: Sketch diagram
Below left: Cutaway perspective rendering through
CTA station tower
Above right: Site diagram
Below right: Axonometric view showing
agricultural plateau

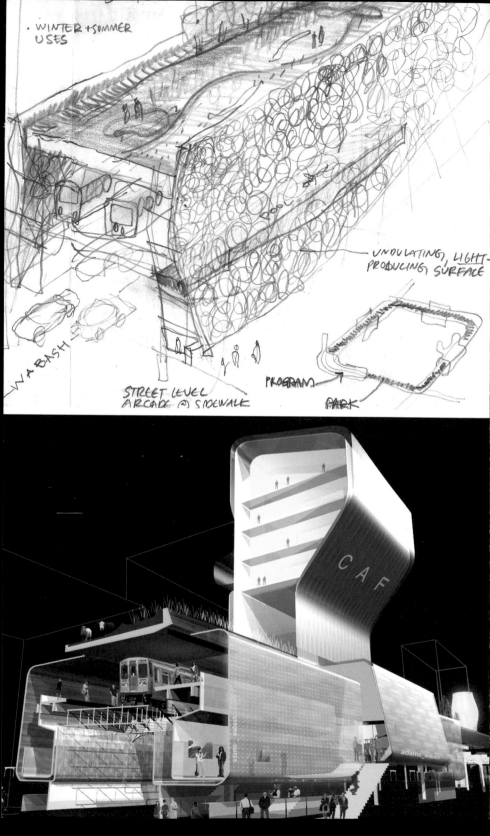

• WINTER + SUMMER
  USES

UNDULATING, LIGHT-
PRODUCING SURFACE

WABASH

STREET LEVEL
ARCADE @ SIDEWALK

PROGRAM

PARK

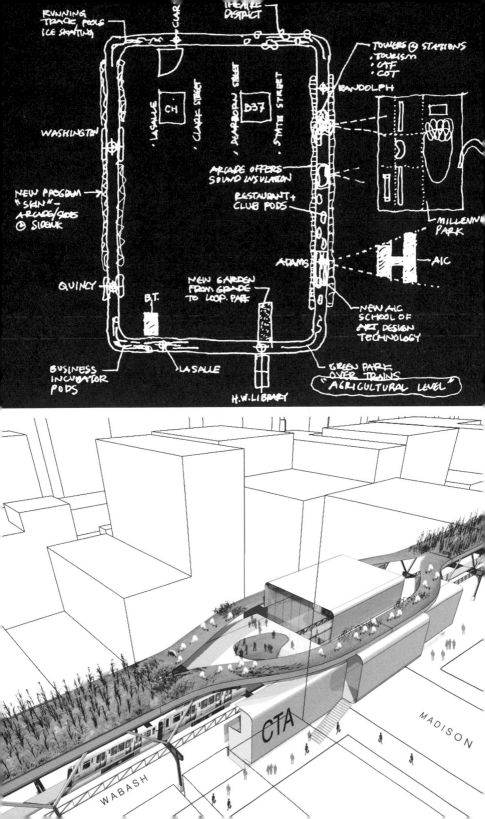

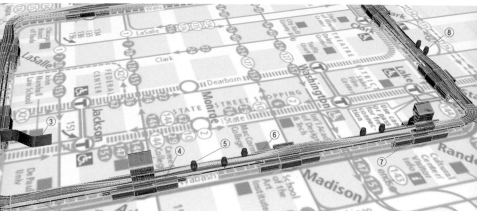

Top: Perspective rendering of agricultural plateau as
seen from nearby office
Above: Axonometric schematic diagram

Perspective rendering of agricultural plateau
and CTA station tower

Jalisco State Public Library

Guadalajara, Mexico, 2005

Garofalo's competition entry for the Jalisco State Public Library in Guadalajara, Mexico, is conceived as a networked, multilayered space that accommodates a variety of user groups and media. The exterior of the library is a relatively simple volume permeated with complex, integrated fields of structural and programmatic forms. The overlapping organization of the landscape elements, the book stacks, and the circulation routes, as well as the building's vertical structure and envelope, facilitates access to information but also allows visitors to meander through the space and use the plan of the library itself as a learning experience.

The landscape north and south of the library guides visitors inside with an undulating surface reminiscent of the dunes that lie north of Guadalajara. The stacks and structural columns create fields of discrete objects regularly and irregularly punctuating the main body of the building. Among these forms, circulation paths cut across the functional boundaries of the library, bringing visitors into contact with a variety of services and features. Vernacular materials like brick and terracotta form an exterior building envelope that reflects the internal, programmatic conditions. Garofalo used computer modeling to determine the final form for these traditional materials; the software allowed him to optimize the shading and natural light for each interior space with pixelated patterns that shift with the changing light.

COMMUNITARIAN ACTIVITIES - CULTURAL & SCIENTIFIC EXPRESSION

EDUCATION FOR LIFE - COMMUNITY INFORMATION CENTER - PUBLIC WORKING SPACE REGARDING READING - RESEARCH ARCHIVE

GENERAL LIBRARY - SUPPORT CENTER FOR FORMAL EDUCATION - REFERENCE CENTER - ACCESS TO THE INFORMATION HIGHWAY

LEARNING DOOR FOR CHILDREN - ECONOMIC INCUBATION REFERRAL CENTER

NON ASSIGNED AREAS

GATHERING POINTS

PLACES FOR

COLLECTIONS

USER

SPECIAL USE SPACES

SPECIAL USE SPACES

PLACES TO PERSON

TRADITIONAL & DIGITAL SERVICES
LOCAL RESEARCHERS
AREAS FOR INFORMAL READING
INTERNATIONAL RESEARCHERS
SPACES FOR TOYS
AREAS FOR FORMAL READING
HAND WRITTEN COLLECTIONS
HISTORIC INVESTIGATIONS
SPECIAL ATTENTION TO THE YOUNG & DISABLED
RARE DOCUMENTS
ANTIQUE DOCUMENTS
ELECTRONIC ROOMS
DIGITZING
INFORMATIONAL
ALPHABETIZATION
TRAINING
SPACES FOR STORY-TELLING
NATIONAL RESEARCHERS
ELECTRONIC & NEWSPAPER SERVICES
CONSERVE
"YOUR YOUNG SPACE"
FOR TEENAGERS
PRESERVE
"COMMUNITARIAN AREA FOR ELECTRONIC WORK"
READING CLUBS
THEATER
STRENGTHEN CULTURAL IDENTITY
VIDEO ROOM
ARTISTIC WORKSHOP SPACES
BOOK WEALTH
STIMULATE INTELLECTUAL CURIOSITY IN YOUTH
COMMUNITY SPACES
PRINTED COLLECTIONS
JALISCO INDIGENOUS CULTERES CENTER
STORE
EXHIBITION AREAS
MICROFILMING
DIGITIZING
INTERNATIONAL READING CENTER
CYBER CAFE
MEDICAL SERVICES
PHOTOGRAPHIC COLLECTIONS
STATE OF THE ART EQUIPMENT

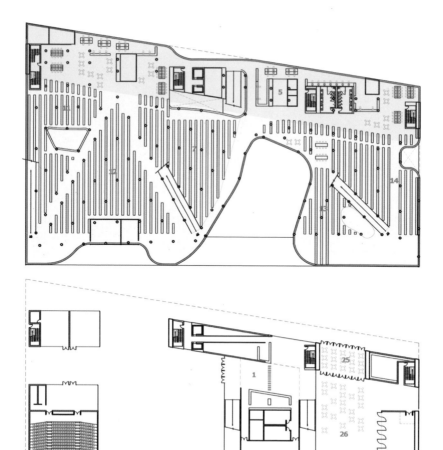

Top: Second-floor plan
Above: First-floor plan

Preceding page: Conceptual diagram

terior perspective views

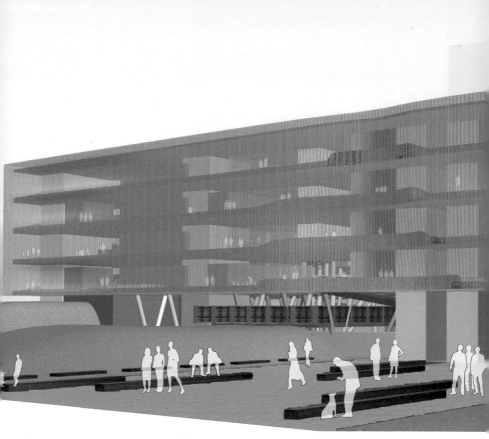

Exterior perspective rendering of north façade

Project Information

Camouflage House
Location: Burr Ridge, Illinois
Design: 1991
Status: unbuilt
Client: Pacific-Sakata Development
Design team: Douglas Garofalo, Jesus Herrarias, David Leary

Markow Residence
Location: Prospect Heights, Illinois
Design: 1995–98
Status: completed
Client: Andrew and Aleksandra Markow
Design team: Douglas Garofalo, Minkyu Whang
Structural engineer: Thornton Tomasetti Engineers

Korean Presbyterian Church of New York
Location: Queens, New York
Design: 1996–99
Status: completed
Client: Korean Presbyterian Church of New York
Design team: Douglas Garofalo, Greg Lynn, Michael McInturf
Structural engineer: FTL/Happold
Mechanical engineer: Lazlo Bodak Engineering

Chicago Public School
Location: Chicago, Illinois
Design: 2000–01
Status: unbuilt; competition entry
Client: Chicago Public Schools
Design team: Douglas Garofalo, Randall Kober, Julie Flohr, Una Moon,

Robert Pontarelli, Carl Karlen
Structural engineer: Thornton Tomasetti Engineers

Manilow Residence
Location: Spring Prairie, Wisconsin
Design: 2000–03
Status: completed
Client: Susan and Lewis Manilow
Design team: Douglas Garofalo, Julie Flohr, Una Moon, Carl Karlen,
Joshua Roberts
Structural engineer: Matrix Engineering
Mechanical engineer: Vorpegel

ABLA Homes
Location: Chicago, Illinois
Design: 2001
Status: unbuilt; second-place competition entry
Client: Chicago Housing Authority and the National Endowment for the
Arts; New Public Works Program
Design team: Douglas Garofalo, Randall Kober,
Julie Flohr, Carl Karlen, Una Moon, Robert Pontarelli, Jeff Morgan,
Joshua Roberts, Steven Eddy
Structural engineer: Thornton Tomasetti Engineers

MCA: Between the Museum and the City
Location: Chicago, Illinois
Design: 2001–02
Status: completed (deinstalled 2003)
Client: Museum of Contemporary Art
Design team: Douglas Garofalo, Randall Kober, Julie Flohr, Carl Karlen,
Una Moon, Christine Garofalo, Will Corcoran, Nicole Covarrubias,
Kenneth Glazer, Colin Morgan, Siamak Mostoufi, Masha Safina, Karla
Sierralta, Brian Strawn, Bill Turoczy
Structural engineer: Thornton Tomasetti Engineers

Nothstine Residence
Location: Green Bay, Wisconsin
Design: 2002–04
Status: completed
Client: Craig and Julie Nothstine
Design team: Douglas Garofalo, Randall Kober, Julie Flohr, Carl Karlen,

Una Moon
Structural engineer: Thornton Tomasetti Engineers

Hyde Park Art Center
Location: Chicago, Illinois
Design: 2002–06
Status: completed
Client: Hyde Park Art Center
Design team: Douglas Garofalo, Andrew Schachman, Grant Gibson,
Randall Kober, Julie Flohr, Carl Karlen, Una Moon, Chris Wolf
Structural engineer: Thornton Tomasetti Engineers
Mechanical engineer: Building Engineering Systems

Pedestrian Bridge
Location: Chicago, Illinois
Design: 2003
Status: schematic design; unbuilt; competition entry
Client: City of Chicago, Department of Transportation, Bureau of Bridges
and Transit
Design team: Douglas Garofalo, Una Moon, Carl Karlen
Structural engineer: URS Corporation

Ford Calumet Environmental Center
Location: Chicago, Illinois
Design: 2003–04
Status: unbuilt; competition entry
Client: City of Chicago, Department of the Environment
Design team: Douglas Garofalo, Xavier Vendrell, Garry Alderman
Structural engineer: Thornton Tomasetti Engineers

Richmond Center for Visual Arts
Location: Kalamazoo, Michigan
Design: 2003–04
Status: completed design development
Client: Western Michigan University
Design team: Douglas Garofalo, Elaine Fitzgerald, Una Moon, Grant
Gibson, Randall Kober, Julie Flohr, Carl Karlen, Garry Alderman
Associate architect: Eckert Wordell, Kalamazoo, Michigan
Structural engineer: Thornton Tomasetti Engineers
Mechanical engineer: Ketchmark + Associates

Gary Residence
Location: Ada, Michigan
Design: 2004–06
Status: under construction
Client: Brian and Melissa Gary
Design team: Douglas Garofalo, Garry Alderman, Kiel Moe, Grant Gibson,
Una Moon, Louis Shell
Structural engineer: Louis Shell Structures
Mechanical engineer: Building Engineering Systems

Griffith Residence
Location: Decatur, Illinois
Design: 2004–06
Status: under construction
Client: Tom and Eva Griffith
Design team: Douglas Garofalo, Garry Alderman, Grant Gibson, Kiel Moe
Structural engineer: Rockey Structures
Mechanical engineer: Building Engineering Systems

New Loop Ecologies
Location: Chicago, Illinois
Design: 2004–05
Status: schematic design; unbuilt
Client: Chicago Central Area Committee
Design team: Douglas Garofalo, Grant Gibson, Garry Alderman

Jalisco State Public Library
Location: Guadalajara, Mexico
Design: 2005
Status: unbuilt; competition entry
Client: Centro Cultural Universitario: Concurso Biblioteca
Design team: Douglas Garofalo, Grant Gibson, Andrew Schachman,
Elaine Fitzgerald, Una Moon, Kiel Moe, Garry Alderman
Structural engineer: Thornton Tomasetti Engineers
Environmental engineer: Atelier 10 Engineers
Lighting engineer: Charter Sills

Selected Bibliography

Amelar, Sarah. 2000. "Garofalo Architects Blows the Roof off a Standard Suburban House with the Markow Residence." **Architectural Record** 188, 1 (January), pp. 104–09.

Coleman, Cindy, and Douglas A. Garofalo. 2002. "IT is It: What Makes Progressive Chicago Architect Doug Garofalo Run? The Latest Technological Developments, for Starters." **Interior Design** 73, 5 (May), pp. 307–09.

Demby, Eric. 2003. "Mellow Yellow: Taking a Cue from P.S. 1, Chicago's Museum of Contemporary Art Lightens up with a Chill-Out Pavilion for Summer." **Metropolis** 23, 1 (August), p. 56.

Garofalo, Douglas A. 1993. "The Camouflage House." **Assemblage** 21 (August), pp. 72–81.

Giovannini, Joseph. 2004. "Computer Worship." **Architecture** 88, 10 (October), pp. 88–99.

Keegan, Edward . 2003. "Garofalo's Temporary Installation Graces Chicago MCA Stairs." **Architectural Record** 191, 6 (June), p. 32.

―――. 2004. "Prairie Poetry: Chicago Architect Doug Garofalo Uses Digital Technology to Remake the American Farmhouse." **Metropolis** 24, 3 (November), pp. 82–89, 125.

McAnulty, Robert. 2001. "Is Chicago 'Merely' History?" **Praxis: Journal of Writing + Building** 3, pp. 63–73.

Museum of Contemporary Art, University of Illinois at Chicago, and Garofalo Architects. 2003. **Between the Museum and the City**. Exh. cat. Museum of Contemporary Art/College of Architecture and the Arts, University of Illinois at Chicago.

Rosa, Joseph. 2001. **Folds, Blobs, and Boxes: Architecture in the Digital Era**. Exh. cat. Heinz Architectural Center, Carnegie Museum of Art, Pittsburgh.

————. 2003. **Next Generation Architecture: Folds, Blobs, and Boxes**. Rizzoli International.

Slessor, Catherine. 2002. "Breaking the Box: House, Chicago, USA." **Architectural Review** 212, 1269 (November), pp. 72–75.

Spiegler, Marc. 1996. "At Play in Peoria." **Metropolis** 15, 10 (June), pp. 54–57, 67.

Tigerman, Stanley, and William Martin, eds. 2005. **Visionary Chicago Architecture: Fourteen Inspired Concepts for the Third Millennia**. Chicago Central Area Committee.